WEEK OF ALL WEEKS

A PRAYER BOOK
FOR HOLY WEEK
AND EASTER DAY

Compiled by Harold Miller

ISBN number: 978-1-904884-52-1 Published in 2015

WEEK OF ALL WEEKS is a prayer book for Holy Week and Easter Day. Its intention is to enliven and enrich our worship experience during that most wonderful and focussed week of the Christian year. In any particular situation, certain parts will be used and others left for the moment. For some people it may also be a book of devotion, helping us to walk through the story in our own personal prayers. Holy Week and Easter tell a story which is dramatic and engaging, and the purpose of these liturgies is that God's people enter fully into the riches of all that has been accomplished for us by Jesus Christ in these focal days of history. A very substantial portion of each of the Gospels is given to the story of this one week, and it is right that we should spend time meditating on the central aspects of our salvation.

This is, in a sense, an informal liturgy book, though it is written very much with the support and encouragement of the Liturgical Advisory Committee, and is built on the liturgical structures, and indeed words of the Book of Common Prayer 2004, and owes a great deal to the Church of England material in Times and Seasons, which has been commended for use by the Church of Ireland bishops.

My prayer is that you will be greatly blessed not only by the services in the book, but by the Lord whom we discover and worship in them.

+ Harold Miller

PALM SUNDAY

THE LITURGY OF THE PALMS

A SERVICE OF THE WORD
(AND HOLY COMMUNION)
FOR PALM SUNDAY

A SERVICE OF READINGS AND
HYMNS FOR PALM SUNDAY EVENING

Palm Sunday begins with a procession - a procession in which everyone may become involved. We begin our Holy Week story as Jesus rides on a donkey into Jerusalem, and the congregation, from the youngest to the oldest, becomes the crowd. It is the first dramatic event in a tumultuous week and offers us a unique opportunity to place ourselves at the scene.

THE LITURGY OF THE PALMS

THE GATHERING OF GOD'S PEOPLE

The presiding minister greets the congregation:
Grace, mercy and peace
from God our Father
and the Lord Jesus Christ
be with you all
and also with you.

Blessed is the King who comes in the Name of the Lord!
Peace in heaven and glory in the highest heaven!
Hosanna to the Son of David, the King of Israel!
Hosanna in the highest!

The service is introduced with these or similar words:
Brothers and sisters in Christ, today begins the week of all weeks. This
is the week in which we follow our Saviour Jesus Christ on the way
of suffering to the Cross and on the way of victory through the Cross
to the Resurrection. Today, we gather with the crowds on the road to
Jerusalem, to greet Our Lord as he begins his journey, to sing his praise
and to welcome him to his city. We rejoice with all our hearts and
voices in the knowledge that, if we do not speak out his praises, the
stones themselves will sing.

O Lord, open our lips
and our mouth will proclaim your praise!

Palm crosses, leaves or branches are distributed to all, then each person
holds up their palm as the following prayer is said:
God our Saviour,
whose Son Jesus Christ entered Jerusalem as Messiah,
to suffer and to die;
let these palms be for us signs of his victory;
and grant that we who bear them in his name,
may ever hail him as our King,
and follow him in the way that leads to eternal life;
who is alive and reigns with you
in the unity of the Holy Spirit,
one God now and for ever. Amen.

THE GOSPEL

The Gospel for the Liturgy of the Palms
In Year A: Matthew 21: 1-11
In Year B: Mark 11: 1-11
In Year C: Luke 19: 28-40

THE PSALM
118: 1-2, 19-29

O give thanks to the Lord, for he is good:
his mercy endures forever.

Let Israel now proclaim:
'His mercy endures for ever'.
Open to me the gates of righteousness
that I may enter and give thanks to the Lord
This is the gate of the Lord:
the righteous shall enter through it.
O give thanks to the Lord for he is good:
his mercy endures forever.

I will give thanks to you, for you have answered me:
and have become my salvation.
The stones which the builders rejected:
have become the chief cornerstone.
This is the Lord's doing:
and it is marvellous in our eyes.
O give thanks to the Lord for he is good:
his mercy endures forever.

This is the day that the Lord has made:
we will rejoice and be glad in it.
Come, O Lord, and save us we pray:
come, Lord, send us now prosperity.
O give thanks to the Lord for he is good:
his mercy endures forever.

Blessed is he who comes in the name of the Lord:
we bless you from the house of the Lord.
The Lord is God; he has given us light:
link the pilgrims with cords, right to the horns of the altar.
O give thanks to the Lord for he is good:
his mercy endures forever.

You are my God and I will thank you:
you are my God and I will exalt you.
O give thanks to the Lord for he is good:
his mercy endures forever.

The minister says:
Let us go forth, praising Jesus our Messiah.

The musicians now lead the procession, waving their palms,
and repeating:
Blessed is he who comes in the name of the Lord!
Hosanna in the highest!

A SERVICE OF THE WORD
(AND HOLY COMMUNION)
FOR PALM SUNDAY MORNING

The congregation gathers in the church

A hymn or other suitable music is played

The large palms at the front of the procession are placed
visibly for all to see.

**THE COLLECT OF
PALM SUNDAY**

Almighty and everlasting God,
who, in your tender love towards the human race,
sent your Son, our Saviour Jesus Christ,
to take upon him our flesh,
and to suffer death upon the cross,
Grant that we may follow the example
of his patience and humility,
and also be made partakers of his resurrection,
through Jesus Christ our Lord. **Amen.**

PROCLAIMING AND RECEIVING THE WORD

READINGS

Either one or two readings from scripture precede the Gospel reading

**THE PASSION
GOSPEL**

The Passion Gospel may be read as a dramatized reading. (See page 84)

The Gospel is introduced with the words:
The Passion of our Lord Jesus Christ, according to...

At the end, the reader says
This is the Passion of the Lord.
A period of silence is kept for reflection

**SERMON OR
MEDITATION**

THE PRAYERS OF THE PEOPLE

The Palm Sunday Intercessions on page 86 may be used

PRAYERS OF
INTERCESSION

Once we were far off
but now we have been brought near
through the shedding of Christ's blood,
for he is our peace.

THE PEACE

The peace of the Lord be always with you
and also with you.

If Holy Communion does not follow, the service ends with the Lord's
Prayer followed by the Blessing and the Dismissal (page 12)

When Holy Communion is celebrated, the service continues with:

CELEBRATING AT THE LORD'S TABLE

This Prayer may be said:
Jesus, true vine and bread of life,
ever giving yourself that the world might live,
let us share your death and passion,
make us perfect in your love. **Amen.**

THE PREPARATION
OF THE TABLE

The Lord is here.
His Spirit is with us.
or
The Lord be with you
and also with you.

THE TAKING OF THE
BREAD AND WINE

Lift up your hearts.
We lift them to the Lord.
Let us give thanks to the Lord our God.

THE GREAT
THANKSGIVING
PRAYER 1

THE GREAT
THANKSGIVING
PRAYER 1 (CONT)

It is right to give our thanks and praise.

Father, almighty and everliving God,
at all times and in all places
it is right to give you thanks and praise:
through Jesus Christ our Saviour,
who, for the redemption of the world,
humbled himself to death on the cross;
that, being lifted up from the earth,
he might draw all people to himself:
and so with all your people,
with angels and archangels,
and with all the company of heaven,
we proclaim your great and glorious name,
for ever praising you and saying:
Holy, holy, holy Lord,
God of power and might,
heaven and earth are full of your glory.
Hosanna in the highest!
Blessed is he who comes in the name of the Lord.
Hosanna in the highest!

Blessed are you, Father,
the creator and sustainer of all things;
you made us in your own image,
male and female you created us;
even when we turned away from you,
you never ceased to care for us,
but in your love and mercy you freed us from the slavery of sin,
giving your only begotten Son to become man
and suffer death on the cross to redeem us:
he made there the one complete and all-sufficient sacrifice
for the sins of the whole world:
he instituted, and in his holy Gospel commanded us to continue,
a perpetual memory of his precious death
until he comes again.
On the night that he was betrayed he took bread;
and when he had given thanks to you, he broke it,
and gave it to his disciples, saying, Take, eat,
this is my body which is given for you.
Do this in remembrance of me.

In the same way, after supper he took the cup;
and when he had given thanks to you,
he gave it to them, saying, Drink this, all of you,
for this is my blood of the new covenant
which is shed for you and for many
for the forgiveness of sins.
Do this, as often as you drink it,
in remembrance of me.

Therefore, Father, with this bread and this cup
we do as Christ your Son commanded:
we remember his passion and death,
we celebrate his resurrection and ascension,
and we look for the coming of his kingdom.

Accept through him, our great high priest,
this our sacrifice of praise and thanksgiving;
and as we eat and drink these holy gifts,
grant by the power of the life-giving Spirit
that we may be made one in your holy Church
and partakers of the body and blood of your Son,
that he may dwell in us and we in him:

Through the same Jesus Christ our Lord,
by whom, and with whom, and in whom,
in the unity of the Holy Spirit,
all honour and glory are yours, Almighty Father,
for ever and ever. Amen.

As our Saviour Christ has taught us, so we pray
Our Father in heaven...
or
As our Saviour Christ has taught us, we are bold to say
Our Father, who art in heaven...

THE LORD'S PRAYER

Every time we eat this bread and drink this cup,
we proclaim the Lord's death until he comes.

THE BREAKING OF
THE BREAD

AGNUS DEI

Jesus, Lamb of God, have mercy on us,
Jesus, bearer of our sins, have mercy on us,
Jesus, Redeemer of the world, grant us peace.

THE COMMUNION

Jesus Christ is the Lamb of God
who has taken away the sins of the world.
Happy are those who are called to his supper:
Lord, I am not worthy to receive you,
but only say the word and I shall be healed.

THE GREAT SILENCE

GOING OUT AS GOD'S PEOPLE

PRAYER AFTER COMMUNION

Lord Jesus Christ,
you humbled yourself in taking the form of a servant
and in obedience died on the cross for our salvation.
Give us the mind to follow you
and to proclaim you as Lord and King,
to the glory of God the Father. Amen.

THE BLESSING

May the Father,
who so loved the world he gave his only Son,
bring you by faith to his eternal life.
Amen.
May Christ,
who accepted the cup of sacrifice
in obedience to the Father's will,
keep you steadfast as you walk with him the way of his cross.
Amen.

May the Spirit,
who strengthens us to suffer with Christ
that we may share his glory,
set your minds on life and peace.
Amen. [1]

And the blessing ...

Walk with Christ this week in the way of his cross and resurrection:
Thanks be to God.

A SERVICE OF READINGS AND HYMNS

FOR PALM SUNDAY EVENING
following the Passion according to Luke

OPENING HYMN

INTRODUCTION

Brothers and sisters in Christ, we stand this Sunday evening at the gateway of the week of all weeks, in which our Lord Jesus won for us our salvation. The story of this week is a story of real events two thousand years ago, but it is also the story which gives meaning to our lives and faith here and now. So, we not only walk with Jesus in these days of his suffering, but we also ask him to give us grace to receive all he has accomplished for us in his bitter passion and death, and to enable us also to walk faithfully with our God in the way which leads to life and peace.

COLLECT

Let us pray.
Almighty and everlasting God,
who, in your tender love towards the human race,
sent your Son, our Saviour Jesus Christ
to take upon him our flesh
and to suffer death upon the cross:
Grant that we may follow the example of his patience and humility,
and also be made partakers of his resurrection;
through Jesus Christ our Lord. **Amen.**

Meditative instrumental music

THE READINGS AND HYMNS

I
Reading 1: Luke 14: 25-33
The cost of discipleship
Hymn

II
Reading 2: Luke 18: 31-34
Jesus foretells his death and resurrection
Instrumental music, song or anthem

III
Reading 3: Luke 19: 28-44
Jesus' triumphal entry into Jerusalem and weeping over the city
Hymn

IV

Reading 4: Luke 19: 45- 20:8
Jesus cleanses the temple
Hymn

V

Reading 5: Luke 20: 9-18
The parable of the wicked tenants
Instrumental music, song or anthem

VI

Reading 6: Luke 22: 1-23
The plot to kill Jesus and the Passover
Hymn

VII

Reading 7: Luke 22: 31-62
Peter's denial and the Mount of Olives
Hymn

VIII

Reading 8: Luke 22: 63-23:25
The trial and sentencing of Jesus

Instrumental music

IX

Reading 9: Luke 23: 26-49
The Crucifixion
Hymn

The Palm Sunday Intercessions on page 86 may be used

Christ draw you to himself
and grant that you find in his cross
a sure ground for faith,
a firm support for hope,
and the assurance of sins forgiven.

PRAYERS AND
BLESSING

HOLY WEEK LITURGIES

AN ORDER FOR HOLY COMMUNION FOR
USE DURING HOLY WEEK

———————

A SERVICE OF THE WORD FOR USE ON
THE MONDAY OF HOLY WEEK

———————

A SERVICE OF THE WORD FOR USE ON
THE TUESDAY OF HOLY WEEK

———————

A SERVICE OF THE WORD FOR USE ON
THE WEDNESDAY OF HOLY WEEK

The first days of Holy Week set the scene for what is to come in the three days between the Last Supper on Maundy Thursday evening and the joyful resurrection on Easter morning. The introductions to the evening services tell of some of the key parts of the story which have been remembered on these days. It is wonderful if we can see them as a journey in our own spiritual lives: an opportunity for devotion, an opening of ourselves to the will and purpose of Christ, and as a way of standing with him as his disciples, as he goes through the events which lead to our reconciliation with God.

AN ORDER FOR HOLY COMMUNION

FOR USE DURING HOLY WEEK

from Monday to Thursday morning

THE GATHERING OF GOD'S PEOPLE

The Lord of love be with you
and also with you

THE GREETING

This is love, not that we loved God, but that he loved us and sent his son as an atoning sacrifice for our sins. *1 John 4: 10 TNIV*

SENTENCE OF SCRIPTURE

O Saviour of the world,
by your cross and precious blood you have redeemed us;
save us and help us, we humbly pray, O Lord. Amen

OPENING PRAYER

Silence

The Beatitudes may be said in preparation for the Confession
Let us hear God's blessing on those who follow him:

PENITENCE

Blessed are the poor in spirit,
for theirs is the kingdom of heaven.
Jesus, remember me
when you come into your kingdom.

Blessed are the meek,
for they shall inherit the earth.
Jesus, remember me
when you come into your kingdom.

Blessed are those who weep
for they shall be consoled.
Jesus, remember me
when you come into your kingdom.

PENITENCE (CONT)

Blessed are those who hunger and thirst after justice,
for they shall be satisfied.
Jesus, remember me
when you come into your kingdom.

Blessed are the merciful,
for they shall obtain mercy.
Jesus, remember me
when you come into your kingdom.

Blessed are the pure in heart
for they shall see God.
Jesus, remember me
when you come into your kingdom.

Blessed are the peacemakers,
for they shall be called the children of God.
Jesus, remember me
when you come into your kingdom.

Blessed are those who suffer persecution
for the sake of justice,
for theirs is the kingdom of heaven.
Jesus, remember me
when you come into your kingdom.

CONFESSION

Trusting in the death and resurrection of our Lord Jesus Christ, we
confess our weakness, our disobedience and our sinfulness, assured that
through the Cross we are completely forgiven:

Gracious and merciful God
as in heart and mind we see Jesus in his passion,
we confess our sins of thought, word and deed,
and our failure to do what we know we should.
Our sins, with those of all humankind,
brought him to the cross:
we are indeed sorry
and are overwhelmed by your wonderful love
by which we receive forgiveness.
Guide and strengthen us to amend our lives

and become disciples worthy of your love.
We ask this through him who suffered and died for us
and now lives with you in the fullness of glory,
Jesus Christ our Lord. Amen. [2]

Priest
Christ Jesus came into the world to save sinners.
Hear then the word of grace and the assurance of pardon.
Your sins are forgiven through his Name.

ABSOLUTION

Almighty God,
whose most dear Son went not up to joy,
but first he suffered pain,
and entered not into glory before he was crucified:
Mercifully grant that we,
walking in the way of his cross,
may find it none other than the way of life and peace;
through Jesus Christ our Lord. **Amen**

THE COLLECT OF THE DAY (MONDAY)

O God,
who by the passion of your blessed Son
made an instrument of shameful death
to be for us the means of life:
Grant us so to glory in the cross of Christ,
that we may gladly suffer pain and loss
for the sake of your Son our Saviour Jesus Christ,
who lives and reigns with you and the Holy Spirit,
one God, now and for ever. **Amen**

THE COLLECT OF THE DAY (TUESDAY)

Lord God,
whose blessed Son our Saviour
gave his back to the smiters,
and did not hide his face from shame:
Give us grace to endure the sufferings
of this present time,
with sure confidence in the glory that shall be revealed;
through Jesus Christ your Son our Lord. **Amen**

THE COLLECT OF THE DAY (WEDNESDAY)

THE COLLECT OF THE DAY (THURSDAY)

God our Father,
you have invited us to share in the supper
which your Son gave to his Church
to proclaim his death until he comes:
may he nourish us by his presence
and unite us in his love:
who is alive and reigns with you and the Holy Spirit,
one God, now and for ever. **Amen.**

PROCLAIMING AND RECEIVING THE WORD

READINGS

The Readings of the Day are used,
The Psalm may be said

The Passion Gospel may be preceded by:
Praise to you, O Christ, King of eternal glory.
Christ humbled himself and became obedient unto death, even death on a cross.
Therefore God has highly exalted him
and given him the name that is above every name:
Praise to you, O Christ, King of eternal glory. [3]

THE PASSION GOSPEL

The Passion Gospel is introduced by the following words without responses:
The Passion of our Lord Jesus Christ, according to...
and concludes with:
This is the Passion of the Lord

After the Gospel a period of silence is kept

THE SERMON

This may appropriately be the reading of a meditation suitable for Holy Week

Silence may be kept

THE PRAYERS OF THE PEOPLE

One of the forms of prayers for Monday-Thursday in Holy Week on pages 87-90 may be used.

Once we were far off,
but now in union with Christ Jesus we have been brought near through the shedding of Christ's blood,
for he is our peace. *Ephesians 2: 13-14*

THE PEACE

The peace of the Lord be always with you:
and also with you.

CELEBRATING AT THE LORD'S TABLE

THE TAKING OF THE BREAD AND WINE

The Lord is here
His Spirit is with us.
or
The Lord be with you
and also with you.

THE GREAT THANKSGIVING PRAYER 2

Lift up your hearts.
We lift them to the Lord.

Let us give thanks to the Lord our God.
It is right to give our thanks and praise.

All glory and honour, thanks and praise
be given to you at all times and in all places,
Lord, holy Father, true and living God,
through Jesus Christ our Lord.

For he is your eternal Word
through whom you have created all things
from the beginning
and formed us in your own image.

In your great love you gave him
to be made man for us and to share our common life.

In obedience to your will
your Son our Saviour offered himself as a perfect sacrifice,
and died on the cross for our redemption.
Through him you have freed us from the slavery of sin
and reconciled us to yourself, our God and Father.

For he is the true Passover Lamb
who was offered for us
and has taken away the sin of the world.
He is our great high priest
whom you raised from death
and exalted to your right hand on high
where he ever lives to intercede for us.

Through him you have sent upon us
your holy and life-giving Spirit
and made us a royal priesthood
called to serve you for ever.

Therefore with angels and archangels
and with all the company of heaven
we proclaim your great and glorious name,
for ever praising you and saying:
Holy, holy, holy Lord,
God of power and might,
heaven and earth are full of your glory.
Hosanna in the highest.

Merciful Father, we thank you
for these gifts of your creation, this bread and this wine,
and we pray that we who eat and drink them
in the fellowship of the Holy Spirit
in obedience to our Saviour Christ

in remembrance of his death and passion
may be partakers of his body and his blood,
who on the night he was betrayed took bread;
and when he had given you thanks
he broke it, and gave it to his disciples, saying,
Drink from this, all of you.
This is my blood of the new covenant
which is shed for you and for many
for the forgiveness of sins.
Do this, as often as you drink it, in remembrance of me.

Father, with this bread and cup,
we do as our Saviour has commanded:
we celebrate the redemption he has won for us;
we proclaim his perfect sacrifice,
made once for all upon the cross,
his mighty resurrection and glorious ascension;
and we look for his coming
to fulfil all things according to your will.
Christ has died;
Christ is risen;
Christ will come again.

Renew us by your Holy Spirit,
unite us in the body of your Son,
and bring us with all your people
into the joy of your eternal kingdom;
through Jesus Christ our Lord,
with whom and in whom,
by the power of the Holy Spirit,
we worship you, Father almighty,
in songs of never-ending praise:
Blessing and honour and glory and power
are yours for ever and ever. Amen.

As our Saviour Christ has taught us, so we pray:
Our Father in heaven...
or
As our Saviour Christ has taught us, we are bold to say:
Our Father, who art in heaven....

THE LORD'S PRAYER

THE BREAKING OF THE BREAD

The bread which we break
is a sharing in the body of Christ.
**We being many are one body,
for we all share in the one bread.**

AGNUS DEI

Lamb of God, you take away the sin of the world
have mercy on us.
Lamb of God, you take away the sin of the world
have mercy on us.
Lamb of God, you take away the sin of the world
grant us peace.

THE COMMUNION

Jesus Christ is the Lamb of God,
who has taken away the sins of the world.
happy are those who are called to his supper.
**Lord, I am not worthy to receive you,
but only say the word and I shall be healed.**

Draw near with faith.

The presiding minister and people receive communion

THE GREAT SILENCE

GOING OUT AS GOD'S PEOPLE

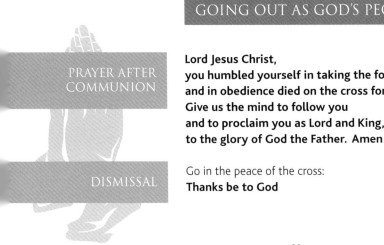

PRAYER AFTER COMMUNION

**Lord Jesus Christ,
you humbled yourself in taking the form of a servant
and in obedience died on the cross for our salvation.
Give us the mind to follow you
and to proclaim you as Lord and King,
to the glory of God the Father. Amen**

DISMISSAL

Go in the peace of the cross:
Thanks be to God

A SERVICE OF THE WORD
FOR USE ON THE MONDAY OF HOLY WEEK

PREPARATION

May the grace, healing and forgiveness of the Lord
be with you this Holy Week,
and also with you.

GREETING

**O Saviour of the world,
by your cross and your precious blood you have redeemed us:
save us and help us, we humbly pray. Amen**

OPENING PRAYER

The presiding minister introduces the service with these or other suitable words:
We gather together this evening to continue our journey with the Lord through this Holy Week of our salvation. The Monday in Holy Week is the day on which we remember Jesus overturning the tables of the money-changers in the temple precincts. This is a reminder to us that God's house is always to be essentially a house of prayer. So we ask God to give us pure hearts, devoted to him, that his voice may be clearly heard, and that our priorities this week would be the priorities of Jesus Christ.

INTRODUCTION

Silence

OPENING HYMN

Lord God, you sent your Son to reconcile us to yourself
and one another.
Lord, have mercy
Lord, have mercy

PENITENCE

Lord Jesus, you heal the wounds of sin and division.
Christ, have mercy
Christ, have mercy

Holy Spirit, through you we put to death the sins of the body - and live.
Lord, have mercy
Lord, have mercy

PENITENCE (CONT)

Jesus, Lamb of God, have mercy on us,
Jesus, bearer of our sins, have mercy on us,
Jesus, Redeemer of the world, grant us peace.

THE COLLECT OF THE DAY

Almighty God,
whose most dear Son went not up to joy,
but first he suffered pain,
and entered not into glory before he was crucified:
mercifully grant that we, walking in the way of his cross,
may find it none other than the way of life and peace,
through Jesus Christ our Lord. **Amen**

THE PROCLAIMING AND RECEIVING OF THE WORD

PSALM 36: 5-11

Your love, O Lord, reaches to the heavens,
and your faithfulness to the clouds.

Your righteousness stands like the strong mountains, your justice like
the great deep:
you, Lord, shall save both man and beast.
How precious is your loving mercy, O God:
all mortal flesh shall take refuge under the shadow of your wings.
Your love, O Lord, reaches to the heavens,
and your faithfulness to the clouds.

They shall be satisfied with the abundance of your house: they shall
drink from the river of your delights.
For with you is the well of life:
and in your light shall we see light.
Your love, O Lord, reaches to the heavens,
and your faithfulness to the clouds.

O continue your loving-kindness to those who know you:
and your righteousness to those who are true of heart.
Let not the foot of pride come against me:
nor the hand of the ungodly thrust me away.

Your love, O Lord, reaches to the heavens,
and your faithfulness to the clouds.

Canticle *The Song of Christ's Glory*

Christ Jesus was in the form of God:
but he did not cling to equality with God.
He emptied himself, taking the form of a servant:
and was born in our human likeness.
And being found in human form he humbled himself:
and became obedient unto death, even death on a cross.
Therefore God has highly exalted him:
and bestowed on him the name above every name.
that at the name of Jesus every knee should bow:
in heaven and on earth and under the earth.
and every tongue confess that Jesus Christ is Lord:
to the glory of God the Father. Amen

BIBLE READING

SERMON

THE RESPONSE

A hymn, reflective solo or instrumental music may be used

Christ suffered for us, leaving us an example,
that we should follow in his steps.
He committed no sin, no guile was found on his lips,
when he was reviled, he did not revile in turn.
when he suffered, he did not threaten,
but he trusted himself to God, who judges justly.
Christ himself bore our sins in his body on the tree,
that we might die to sin and live to righteousness.
By his wounds we have been healed, for we were straying like sheep,
but have now returned to the shepherd and guardian of our souls.

SCRIPTURAL
AFFIRMATION
OF FAITH
1 PETER 2: 21B-25

Holy Week Intercessions may be found on pages 87-90

THE PRAYERS

THE LORD'S PRAYER

CLOSING HYMN

BLESSING

Christ draw you to himself
and grant that you find in his cross
a sure ground for faith,
a firm support for hope,
and the assurance of sins forgiven;
and the blessing....

A SERVICE OF THE WORD
FOR USE ON THE TUESDAY OF HOLY WEEK

PREPARATION

May the grace, healing and forgiveness
of the Lord be with you this Holy Week
and also with you.

O Saviour of the world,
by your cross and precious blood you have redeemed us:
save us and help us, we humbly pray. Amen.

The presiding minister introduces the service with these or other
suitable words

We gather together this evening to continue our journey with the Lord
through this Holy Week of our salvation. The Tuesday in Holy Week
is often associated with that scene in the Gospels where a woman
anoints Jesus with precious perfume, as though preparing him for his
death and burial. This is a reminder to us, in this week of all weeks,
that the great love of Jesus, in giving all for us, calls forth our love and
devotion, and our offering of all that is of value to us, not least our
hearts and lives.

Silence

O God, you know my foolishness
and my sins are not hidden from you.
Lord, have mercy
Lord, have mercy

Let not the flood overwhelm me
nor the depths swallow me up:
let not the pit shut its mouth upon me.
Christ, have mercy
Christ, have mercy

Hear me, O Lord, as your loving-kindness is good;
turn to me, as your compassion is great.
Lord, have mercy
Lord, have mercy

Jesus, Lamb of God, have mercy on us,
Jesus, bearer of our sins, have mercy on us,
Jesus, Redeemer of the world, grant us peace.

THE COLLECT OF THE DAY

O God,
who by the passion of your blessed Son
made an instrument of shameful death
to be for us the means of life:
Grant us so to glory in the cross of Christ
that we may gladly suffer pain and loss
for the sake of your Son our Saviour Jesus Christ:
who lives and reigns with you and the Holy Spirit,
one God now and for ever. **Amen**

THE PROCLAIMING AND RECEIVING OF THE WORD

PSALM 71: 1-14

In you, O Lord, do I take refuge
let me never be put to shame.

In your righteousness deliver me and set me free:
incline your ear to me and save me.
Be for me a stronghold to which I may ever resort:
send out to save me, for you are my rock and my fortress.
Deliver me, my God, from the hand of the wicked:
from the grasp of the evildoer and the oppressor.
In you, O Lord, do I take refuge
let me never be put to shame.

For you are my hope, O Lord God;
my confidence, even from my youth.
Upon you have I leaned from my birth,

when you drew me from my mother's womb:
my praise shall be always of you.
In you, O Lord, do I take refuge
let me never be put to shame.

I have become a portent to many:
but you are my refuge and my strength.
Let my mouth be full of your praise:
and your glory all the day long.
Do not cast me away in the time of old age:
forsake me not when my strength fails.
In you, O Lord, do I take refuge
let me never be put to shame.

For my enemies are talking against me:
and those who lie in wait for my life take counsel together: They say
'God has forsaken him; pursue him and take him:
because there is none to deliver him'.
In you, O Lord, do I take refuge
let me never be put to shame.

O God, be not far from me:
come quickly to help me, O my God.
Let those who are against me be put to shame and disgrace: let those
who seek to do me evil be covered with scorn and reproach,
But as for me, I will hope continually:
and will praise you more and more.
In you, O Lord, do I take refuge
let me never be put to shame.

BIBLE READING

CANTICLE THE
SONG OF ISAIAH

Surely God is my salvation:
I will trust and will not be afraid.
For the Lord God is my strength and my might;
he has become my salvation.
With joy you will draw water from the wells of salvation:
and you will say in that day: Give thanks to the Lord, call on his name;
make known his deeds among the nations:
proclaim that his name is exalted.
Sing praises to the Lord, for he has done gloriously:

let this be known in all the earth.
Shout aloud and sing for joy, O Royal Zion,
for great in your midst is the Holy One of Israel.

Glory to the Father and to the Son, and to the Holy Spirit:
as it was in the beginning is now, and shall be for ever. Amen.

SERMON

THE RESPONSE

Hymn, reflective solo or instrumental music

**SCRIPTURAL
AFFIRMATION
OF FAITH
1 PETER 2: 21B-25**

Christ suffered for us, leaving us an example,
that we should follow in his steps.
He committed no sin, no guile was found on his lips,
when he was reviled, he did not revile in turn.
when he suffered, he did not threaten,
but he trusted himself to God, who judges justly.
Christ himself bore our sins in his body on the tree,
that we might die to sin and live to righteousness.
By his wounds we have been healed, for we were straying like sheep,
but have now returned to the shepherd and guardian of our souls.

THE PRAYERS

Holy Week Intercessions may be found on pages 87-90

THE LORD'S PRAYER

CLOSING HYMN

BLESSING

Christ draw you to himself
and grant that you find in his cross
a sure ground for faith,
a firm support for hope,
and the assurance of sins forgiven;
and the blessing.....

A SERVICE OF THE WORD
FOR USE ON THE WEDNESDAY OF HOLY WEEK

PREPARATION

May the grace, healing and forgiveness of the Lord
be with you this Holy Week
and also with you.

GREETING

**O Saviour of the world,
by your cross and precious blood you have redeemed us:
save us and help us, we humbly pray. Amen**

OPENING PRAYER

The presiding minister introduces the service with these or other
suitable words

INTRODUCTION

We gather together this evening to continue our journey with the Lord
through this Holy Week of our salvation. The Wednesday in Holy Week
sees the gathering gloom of hatred toward our Lord, of deep betrayal in
the heart of Judas, and of determination to be rid of the very One who
carries our future hope and salvation in his person.

Silence

OPENING HYMN

PENITENCE

When we take our ease,
rather than watch with you.
Lord, have mercy
Lord, have mercy

When we bestow a kiss of peace
Yet nurse enmity in our hearts:
Christ, have mercy
Christ, have mercy

When we strike at those who hurt us,
Rather than stretch out our hands to bless:
Lord, have mercy
Lord, have mercy

Jesus, Lamb of God, have mercy on us,
Jesus, bearer of our sins, have mercy on us,
Jesus, Redeemer of the world, grant us peace.

THE COLLECT
OF THE DAY

Lord God,
Whose blessed Son our Saviour
Gave his back to the smiters,
And did not hide his face from shame:
Give us grace to endure the sufferings
of this present time,
With sure confidence in the glory that shall be revealed:
through Jesus Christ your Son our Lord. **Amen.**

THE PROCLAIMING AND RECEIVING OF THE WORD

PSALM 70

You are my help and my deliverer.
O Lord, do not delay.

O God make speed to save me:
O Lord, make haste to help me.
Let those who seek my life be put to shame and confusion: let them be
turned back and disgraced who wish me evil.
You are my help and my deliverer:
O Lord, do not delay.

Let those who mock and deride me:
turn back because of their shame.
But let all who seek you, rejoice and be glad in you:
Let those who love your salvation say always: 'Great is the Lord'!
You are my help and my deliverer:
O Lord, do not delay.

As for me, I am poor and needy:
come to me quickly, O God.
You are my help and my deliverer:
O Lord, do not delay.

He was despised and rejected by others:
a man of suffering and acquainted with infirmity;
and as one from whom others hide their faces:
he was despised and we held him of no account.
Surely he has borne our infirmities:
and carried our diseases;
yet we accounted him stricken;
struck down by God and afflicted;
but he was wounded for our transgressions:
crushed for our iniquities;
upon him was the punishment that made us whole:
and by his bruises we are healed.

All we like sheep have gone astray:
we have all turned to our own way,
and the Lord has laid on him
the iniquity of us all.
[Glory to the Father, and to the Son,
and to the Holy Spirit:
as it was in the beginning, is now
and shall be for ever. Amen.]

SERMON

THE RESPONSE

Hymn, reflective solo or instrumental music

Christ suffered for us, leaving us an example,
that we should follow in his steps.
He committed no sin, no guile was found on his lips,
when he was reviled, he did not revile in turn.
When he suffered, he did not threaten,
but he trusted himself to God, who judges justly.
Christ himself bore our sins in his body on the tree,

SCRIPTURAL
AFFIRMATION
OF FAITH
1 PETER 2: 21B-25

**that we might die to sin and live to righteousness.
By his wounds we have been healed, for we were straying like sheep, but have now returned to the shepherd and guardian of our souls.**

Holy Week Intercessions may be found on pages 87-90

THE PRAYERS

THE LORD'S PRAYER

CLOSING HYMN

BLESSING

Christ draw you to himself
and grant that you find in his cross
a sure ground for faith, a firm support for hope,
and the assurance of sins forgiven;
and the blessing...

MAUNDY THURSDAY
TO EARLY EASTER EVE

THE LORD'S SUPPER AND
THE WASHING OF FEET

———

A GOOD FRIDAY ALL-AGE SERVICE
OF THE JOURNEY

———

A GOOD FRIDAY THREE HOURS SERVICE

———

A GOOD FRIDAY EVENING SERVICE
WITH THE TENEBRAE

Here we arrive at the heart of the matter. The story begins to unfold with a whole series of events and pictures crowding our minds. The Maundy Thursday evening service has so many aspects that it is hard to fit them all in. There is the washing of feet, the high-priestly prayer of Jesus, which becomes the model for our prayer for unity on that night, the Last Supper, the going out into the Garden of Gethsemane, and the challenge to the disciples to stay with him in his suffering.

Then we move to Good Friday, with the denial of Peter, the trial, the road to Calvary, and the three hours on the cross, leading to his burial.

After that, there is the numbness of early Easter Eve, with a sense of gloom on the surface, but the knowledge by faith of what is happening in the background and the realization of the outcome in the resurrection.

THE LORD'S SUPPER AND THE WASHING OF FEET

THE GATHERING OF GOD'S PEOPLE

Grace, mercy and peace
from God our Father and the Lord Jesus Christ
be with you all:
and also with you.

Return to the Lord, God of all mercies,
for a feast of love has been prepared for his own.
**I will bless the Lord at all times,
his praise shall continually be in my mouth**.

O taste and see the goodness of the Lord,
happy are they who take refuge in him.
**O magnify the Lord with me:
and let us exalt his name together.** [4]

THE GREETING

The presiding minister introduces the service with these or other words

INTRODUCTION

On this night, we come with Jesus and his disciples to the Upper
Room, and meet around the Table at the Last Supper. This Passover
meal becomes for us the sacrament of the Lord's body and blood, in
which we feed on him by faith with thanksgiving. At the supper, Jesus
reveals himself as the servant of all, when he takes water and a towel
and washes the disciples' feet, giving us an example of servanthood to
follow. And at the end of the meal, we go out into the darkness of the
Garden of Gethsemane in preparation for the day to come as we walk
with him to the cross of Calvary.

Silence

Our Lord Jesus Christ says:
'If you love me, keep my commandments'.
'Unless I wash you, you have no part in me'.

CONFESSION

Let us confess to Almighty God our sins against his love, and ask him to

CONFESSION (CONT)

cleanse us:
Have mercy on us, O God, in your great goodness:
according to the multitude of your compassion
blot out our offences.
Lord, have mercy
Lord, have mercy

Against you only have we sinned
and done what is evil in your sight.
Christ, have mercy
Christ, have mercy

Purge us from our sin and we shall be clean:
wash us and we shall be whiter than snow.
Lord, have mercy
Lord, have mercy

ABSOLUTION

May the Father forgive *us*
by the death of his Son
and strengthen *us*
to live in the power of the Spirit
all *our* days. **Amen**

Holy God,
holy and strong,
holy and immortal,
have mercy on us.

A HYMN OF PRAISE

THE COLLECT OF THE LAST SUPPER

Almighty God,
at the Last Supper your Son Jesus Christ
washed the disciples' feet
and commanded them to love one another.
Give us humility and obedience to be servants of others
as he was the servant of all:
who gave up his life and died for us,
yet is alive and reigns with you and the Holy Spirit,
one God, now and for ever. **Amen.**

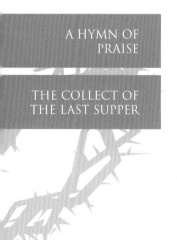

PROCLAIMING AND RECEIVING THE WORD

FIRST READING
EXODUS 12: 1-4 (5-10)

PSALM 116: 1, 10-17

I love the Lord,
for he has heard the voice of his supplication:
because he inclined his ear to me
on the day I called to him.

How shall I repay the Lord:
for all the benefits he has given to me?
I will lift up the cup of salvation:
and call upon the name of the Lord.
I love the Lord,
for he has heard the voice of his supplication:
because he inclined his ear to me
on the day I called to him.

I will fulfil my vows to the Lord:
in the presence of all his people.
Precious in the sight of the Lord:
is the death of his faithful servants.
I love the Lord,
for he has heard the voice of his supplication:
because he inclined his ear to me
on the day I called to him.

O Lord, I am your servant:
your servant, the child of your handmaid:
you have freed me from my bonds.
I will offer you a sacrifice of thanksgiving:
and call upon the name of the Lord.
I love the Lord,
for he has heard the voice of his supplication:
because he inclined his ear to me
on the day I called to him.

I will fulfil my vows to the Lord:
in the presence of all his people,

In the courts of the house of the Lord:
in the midst of you, O Jerusalem. Alleluia.
I love the Lord,
for he has heard the voice of his supplication:
because he inclined his ear to me
on the day I called to him.

SECOND READING
1 CORINTHIANS
11: 23-26

GRADUAL HYMN

This declaration may herald the Gospel Reading

Praise to you, O Christ, King of eternal glory.
I give you a new commandment, says the Lord:
Love one another as I have loved you.
Praise to you, O Christ, King of eternal glory. [5]

GOSPEL
JOHN 13: 1-17: 31B-35

When it is announced:
Glory to you, Lord Jesus Christ

At the end:
Praise to you, Lord Jesus Christ

SERMON

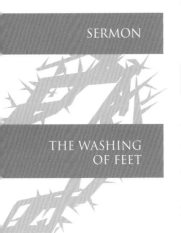

THE WASHING OF FEET AND THE PRAYERS

THE WASHING
OF FEET

The Presiding Minister and others may wash the feet of some members
of the congregation.

The washing of feet may end with the prayer:
Lord Jesus Christ,
you have taught us

that what we do for the least of our brothers and sisters
we do also for you:
give us the will to be the servant of others
as you were the servant of all,
and gave up your life and died for us,
but are alive and reign now and for ever. **Amen.** [6]

In the power of the Spirit let us pray to the Father,
through Christ the Saviour of the world.

Father, on this, the night he was betrayed,
your Son Jesus Christ washed the disciples' feet.
We commit ourselves to follow the example of his love and service.
Lord, hear us
and humble us.

On this night, he prayed for his disciples to be one.
We pray for the unity of your Church.
Lord hear us
and unite us.

On this night, he prayed for those who were to believe through his
disciples' message.
We pray for the mission of your Church.
Lord, hear us
and renew our zeal.

On this night he commanded his disciples to love,
but suffered rejection himself.
We pray for the rejected and unloved.
Lord, hear us
and fill us with your love.

On this night, he reminded his disciples
that, if the world hated them, it hated him first.
We pray for those who are persecuted for their faith.
Lord, hear us
and give us your peace.

On this night, he accepted the cup of death

45

and looked forward to the new wine of the kingdom.
We remember those preparing for death, and ask that they may know the peace of Christ.
Lord, hear us
and welcome all your children into paradise. [7]

THE PEACE

Jesus says: 'Peace I leave with you. My peace I give to you. Do not let your hearts be troubled, neither let them be afraid.'
The peace of the Lord be always with you:
and also with you.

CELEBRATING AT THE LORD'S TABLE

At this eucharist we are with our crucified and risen Lord. We know that it was not only our ancestors, but we who were redeemed, and brought forth from bondage to freedom, from mourning to feasting. We know that as he was with them in the upper room, so our Lord is here with us now.

Until the Kingdom of God comes,
let us celebrate this feast.
Blessed are you Lord, God of the Universe,
you bring forth bread from the earth:
Blessed be God for ever!
Blessed are you Lord, God of the Universe,
you create the fruit of the vine:
Blessed be God for ever! [8]

The presiding minister takes the bread and the wine

The Lord is here
His Spirit is with us
Lift up your hearts
We lift them to the Lord
Let us give thanks to the Lord our God
It is right to give our thanks and praise.

Father, Lord of all creation,
we praise you for your goodness and your love.
When we turned away, you did not reject us.
You came to meet us in your Son,
welcomed us as your children
and prepared a table where we might feast with you.
In Christ you shared our life
that we might live in him and he in us.
He opened wide his arms upon the cross
and, with love stronger than death,
He made the perfect sacrifice for sin.

Lord Jesus Christ, our redeemer,
on this night before you died,
you came to table with your friends.
Taking bread, you gave thanks, broke it,
and gave it to them, saying,
Take, eat: this is my body which is given for you;
do this in remembrance of me.
Lord Jesus, we bless you,
you are the bread of life.

At the end of supper
you took the cup of wine, gave thanks, and said,
Drink this, all of you;
this is my blood of the new covenant,
which is shed for you and for many
for the forgiveness of sins;
do this in remembrance of me.
Lord Jesus, we bless you,
you are the true vine.

Praise to you, Lord Jesus Christ:
dying, you destroyed our death,
Rising, you restored our life;
Lord Jesus, come in glory.

Holy Spirit, giver of life, come upon us now;
may this bread and wine be to us
the body and blood of our Saviour Jesus Christ.
As we eat and drink these holy gifts

**make us, who know our need of grace,
one in Christ, our risen Lord.**

Father, Son, and Holy Spirit, blessed Trinity,
with your whole Church throughout the world
we offer you this sacrifice of thanks and praise
and lift our voice to join the song of heaven,
for ever praising you and saying:
**Holy, holy, holy Lord,
God of power and might,
Heaven and earth are full of your glory,
Hosanna in the highest.**

Thanks be to you, our God, for your gift beyond words.
Amen. Amen. Amen.

**THE LORD'S
PRAYER**

As our Saviour Christ has taught us, so we pray:
Our Father in heaven....
or
As our Saviour Christ has taught us, we are bold to say:
Our Father, who art in heaven...

**THE BREAKING
OF BREAD**

As often as we break this bread and drink this cup
we proclaim the Lord's death until he comes.

AGNUS DEI

Jesus, Lamb of God:
have mercy on us;
Jesus, bearer of our sins:
have mercy on us;
Jesus, Redeemer of the world:
grant us peace.
Silence

COMMUNION

GOING OUT AS GOD'S PEOPLE

Lord Jesus Christ,
in this wonderful sacrament
you have given us a memorial of your passion.
Grant us so to reverence the sacred mysteries
of your body and blood
that we may know within ourselves
the fruits of your redemption,
for you are alive and reign with the Father and the Holy Spirit,
one God, now and for ever. **Amen**

When the disciples had sung a hymn, they went out to the Mount
of Olives. Jesus prayed to the Father: 'If it is possible, Take this cup of
suffering from me'. He said to his disciples, 'How is it that you were not
able to keep watch with me for one hour? The hour has come for the
Son of Man to be handed over to the power of sinners'. [9]

A GOOD FRIDAY MORNING ALL-AGE · SERVICE OF THE JOURNEY[10]

This service takes the shape of the journey of Jesus Christ over the last 24 hours of his earthly life.

INTRODUCTION	The congregation gather in the front seats and the service is briefly explained.
SCENE 1:	The Last Supper
SCENE 2:	The Garden
SCENE 3:	The Courtroom
SCENE 4:	The Hill of Calvary
SCENE 5:	The Tomb

A GOOD FRIDAY THREE HOURS SERVICE

THE SEVEN WORDS FROM THE CROSS

OPENING HYMN

OPENING PRAYER

Lord Jesus Christ,
as you suffered for us on Good Friday,
you spoke your word of grace and truth into the world:
help us so to meditate
on your seven words from the cross,
that we may perceive more deeply
the wonder of our redemption,
for your love and mercy's sake. **Amen.**

I
THE FIRST WORD FROM THE CROSS

'Father, forgive them, for they do not know what they are doing'

At the end of the reading:
God forbid that we should glory
save in the cross of Christ our Lord

READING:
LUKE 23: 32-38

MEDITATION

Lord Jesus Christ,
in your hour of agony,
you asked your Father's forgiveness
for those who caused you pain.
Give us the strength to love our enemies
and bless our persecutors,
that we may reflect your love to those around us,
for your mercy's sake. **Amen.**

PRAYER

Silence

II
THE SECOND WORD FROM THE CROSS:

'Today you will be with me in Paradise'

**READING:
LUKE 23: 39-43**

At the end of the reading:
God forbid that we should glory
save in the cross of Christ our Lord

MEDITATION

PRAYER

Lord Jesus Christ,
you spoke in love to the thief
who asked to be remembered in your kingdom;
Speak the words of eternal life
to all who are sincerely penitent,
with the assurance of being with you in Paradise,
for your mercy's sake. **Amen.**

HYMN

Silence

III
THE THIRD WORD FROM THE CROSS

'Here is your son...here is your mother'

**READING:
JOHN 19: 25-27**

At the end of the reading:
God forbid that we should glory
save in the cross of Christ our Lord

MEDITATION

PRAYER

Lord Jesus Christ,
your mother stayed by your side
faithfully to the very end;
and you, in the midst of your agony, cared for her.
Help us, even when we suffer ourselves,
to see and feel the needs of others

and to act in love towards them,
for your mercy's sake. **Amen.**

HYMN

Silence

IV
THE FOURTH WORD FROM THE CROSS:

'My God, my God, why have you forsaken me?'

At the end of the reading:
God forbid that we should glory
save in the cross of Christ our Lord

READING:
MARK 15: 33-35

MEDITATION

PRAYER

Lord Jesus Christ,
you bore our sins in your body on the tree,
and knew the deep darkness of abandonment;
help us to know your presence when we feel forsaken,
and the wonderful truth that we who were far off
have been brought close by your redeeming blood,
for your mercy's sake. **Amen.**

HYMN

Silence

V
THE FIFTH WORD FROM THE CROSS:

'I am thirsty'

At the end of the reading:
God forbid that we should glory
save in the cross of Christ our Lord

READING:
JOHN 19: 28, 29

MEDITATION

PRAYER

Lord Jesus Christ,
you thirsted physically on the cross
that our spiritual thirst might be quenched.
Draw us ever deeper into the living wells of our salvation
that we may long more and more
for the things of the Spirit,
for your mercy's sake. **Amen.**

HYMN

Silence

VI
THE SIXTH WORD FROM THE CROSS:

'It is finished'

**READING:
JOHN 19: 30-37**

At the end of the reading:
God forbid that we should glory
save in the cross of Christ our Lord

MEDITATION

PRAYER

Lord Jesus Christ,
you were obedient to the very end,
and completed on the cross
the plan of our salvation.
Help us to rejoice in the victory
of your finished work,
and to live out your will and purpose
to the end of our days,
for your mercy's sake. **Amen.**

HYMN

Silence

VII
THE SEVENTH WORD FROM THE CROSS

'Into your hands I commend my spirit'

READING:
LUKE 23: 44-49

MEDITATION

PRAYER

HYMN

At the end of the reading:
God forbid that we should glory
save in the cross of Christ our Lord

Lord Jesus Christ,
in your last word from the cross
you commended your spirit to the Father.
Help us to end our days
in the secure knowledge of your love,
that whether dying or living,
we may be safe in his eternal arms,
for your mercy's sake. **Amen.**

Silence

THE REPROACHES

The Reproaches may be said

Is it nothing to you, all you who pass by?
Look and see if there is any sorrow like my sorrow
which was brought upon me,
which the Lord inflicted on the day of his fierce anger.
Holy God,
holy and strong,
holy and immortal
have mercy upon us.

O my people, O my Church, what have I done to you
or in what have I offended you?
Testify against me.

I led you forth from the land of Egypt, and delivered you by the waters
of baptism, but you have prepared a cross for your Saviour.
Holy God,
holy and strong,
holy and immortal
have mercy upon us

I led you through the desert forty years, and fed you with manna.
I brought you through tribulation and penitence,
and gave you my body, the bread of heaven,
but you prepared a cross for your Saviour.
Holy God,
holy and strong,
holy and immortal
have mercy upon us

What more could I have done for you that I have not done?
I planted you, my chosen and fairest vineyard,
I made you the branches of my vine:
but when I was thirsty, you gave me vinegar to drink,
and pierced with a spear the side of your Saviour.
Holy God,
holy and strong,
holy and immortal
have mercy upon us

I went before you in a pillar of cloud,
and you have led me to the judgement hall of Pilate.
I scourged your enemies and brought you into
a land of freedom, but you have scourged, mocked and beaten me.
I gave you the water of salvation from the rock,
but you have given me gall and left me to thirst.
Holy God,
holy and strong,
holy and immortal
have mercy upon us.

I gave you a royal sceptre, and bestowed the keys of the kingdom,
but you have given me a crown of thorns.
I raised you on high with great power,
but you have hanged me on the cross.

Holy God,
holy and strong,
holy and immortal
have mercy upon us.

My peace I gave, which the world cannot give,
and washed your feet as a sign of my love,
but you draw the sword to strike in my name,
and seek high places in my kingdom.
I offered you my body and my blood
but you scatter and deny and abandon me.
Holy God,
holy and strong,
holy and immortal
have mercy upon us.

I sent the Spirit of truth to guide you,
and you close your hearts to the Counsellor.
I pray that all may be one in the Father and me,
but you continue to quarrel and divide.
I call you to go and bring forth fruit,
but you cast lots for my clothing.
Holy God,
holy and strong,
holy and immortal
have mercy upon us.

I came to you as the least of your brothers and sisters;
I was hungry and you gave me no food,
I was thirsty and you gave me no drink,
I was a stranger and you did not welcome me,
naked and you did not clothe me,
sick and in prison and you did not visit me.
Holy God,
holy and strong,
holy and immortal
have mercy upon us. [11]

CLOSING PRAYER

A GOOD FRIDAY EVENING SERVICE WITH THE TENEBRAE

Silence

The congregation is called to complete silence in preparation for worship. The silence should last for a substantial period of time.

ENTRY OF THE CROSS

A large wooden cross is carried in at the back of the church. Three large nails may be hammered into the wood of the cross, deliberately and firmly.

The cross is carried to the front of the church, and displayed in a central place for all to see. The following acclamations may be used:

We adore you, O Christ, and we bless you,
because by your holy cross you have redeemed the world.

This is the wood of the cross,
on which hung the Saviour of the world.
come, let us worship.

O Saviour of the world,
Who by your cross and precious blood has redeemed us,
save us and help us we humbly pray.

Father, hear our prayer and forgive us.
Unstop our ears,
that we may receive the gospel of the cross.
Lighten our eyes,
that we may see your glory in the face of your Son.
Penetrate our minds,
that your truth may make us whole.
Irradiate our hearts with your love,
that we may love one another for Christ's sake.
Father, forgive us.

THE PREACHING OF THE PASSION

Almighty Father,
look with mercy on this your family
for which our Lord Jesus Christ
was content to be betrayed
and given up into the hands of sinners
and to suffer death upon the cross;
who is alive and glorified with you and the Holy Spirit,
one God, now and for ever. **Amen.**

My God, my God, why have you forsaken me?

My God, my God, why have you forsaken me:
and are so far from my salvation, from the words of my distress?
O my God, I cry in the daytime, but you do not answer:
and by night also, but I find no rest.
Yet you are the Holy One:
enthroned upon the praises of Israel.
Our forebears trusted in you:
they trusted, and you delivered them.
They cried out to you and were delivered:
they put their trust in you and were not confounded.
My God, my God, why have you forsaken me?

But as for me, I am a worm and no man:
scorned by all and despised by the people.
All who see me laugh me to scorn:
they curl their lips and wag their heads, saying,
'He trusted in the Lord, let him deliver him:
let him deliver him, if he delights in him.'
But it is you that took me out of the womb:
and laid me safe upon my mother's breast.
On you was I cast ever since I was born:
you are my God even from my mother's womb.
Be not far from me, for trouble is near at hand:

and there is none to help.
My God, my God, why have you forsaken me?

Mighty oxen come around me:
fat bulls of Bashan close me in on every side.
They gape upon me with their mouths:
as it were a rampaging and a roaring lion.
I am poured out like water; all my bones are out of joint:
my heart has become like wax melting in the depths of my body.
My mouth is dried up like a potsherd; my tongue cleaves to my gums:
you have laid me in the dust of death.
For the hounds are all about me, the pack of evildoers close in on me:
they pierce my hands and my feet.
My God, my God, why have you forsaken me?

I can count all my bones;
they stand staring and looking upon me.
They divide my garments among them:
they cast lots for my clothing.
Be not far from me, O Lord:
you are my strength, hasten to help me.
Deliver my soul from the sword,
my poor life from the power of the dog.
Save me from the lion's mouth:
from the horns of wild oxen. You have answered me.
My God, my God, why have you forsaken me?

I will tell of your name to my people:
in the midst of the congregation will I praise you.
Praise the Lord, you that fear him:
O seed of Jacob, glorify him; stand in awe of him, O seed of Israel.
For he has not despised nor abhorred the suffering of the poor; neither
has he hidden his face from them:
but when they cried to him he heard them.
My God, my God, why have you forsaken me?

From you comes my praise in the great congregation:
I will perform my vows in the presence of those that fear you.
The poor shall eat and be satisfied:
those who seek the Lord shall praise him; their hearts shall live for ever.
All the ends of the earth shall remember and turn to the Lord:

and all the families of the nations shall bow before him.
For the kingdom is the Lord's:
and he rules over the nations.
My God, my God, why have you forsaken me?

How can those who sleep in the earth bow down in worship:
or those who go down to the dust kneel before him?
He has saved my life for himself; my descendants shall serve him:
this shall be told of the Lord for generations to come.
They shall come and make known his salvation, to a people yet unborn:
declaring that he, the Lord, has done it.
My God, my God, why have you forsaken me?

BIBLE READING

PREACHING
THE PASSION

INSTRUMENTAL
MUSIC

HYMN

During this time, the congregation may be encouraged to bring prayers, written on paper or sticky-notes and place them on the cross; or a nail which has been given at the beginning of the service, to place near the cross, as a sign of Christ bearing our sins.

THE TENEBRAE

The congregation is seated and the church is plunged into darkness, apart from the tenebrae candles.

At the end of the tenebrae, when the Christ-candle is re-lit, the congregation sings a Good Friday hymn in the darkness.

The lights are gradually lit, and the congregation leaves in silence.

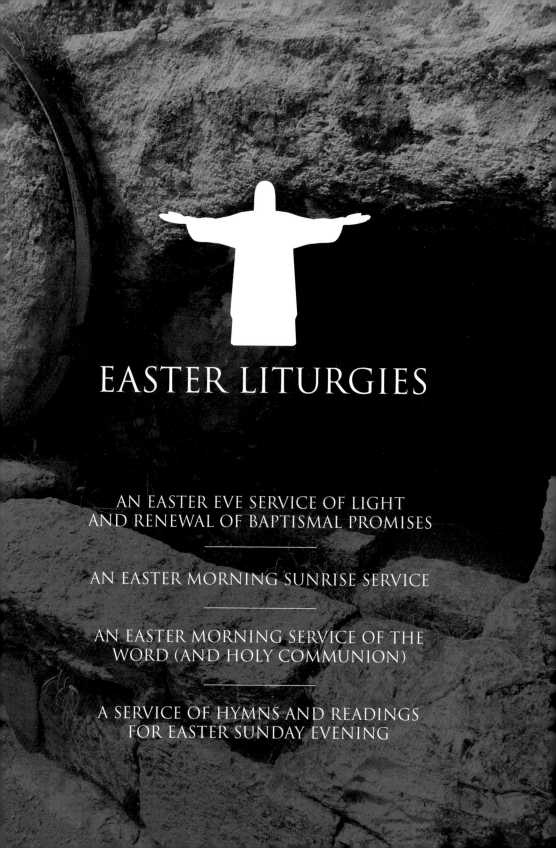

EASTER LITURGIES

AN EASTER EVE SERVICE OF LIGHT
AND RENEWAL OF BAPTISMAL PROMISES

AN EASTER MORNING SUNRISE SERVICE

AN EASTER MORNING SERVICE OF THE
WORD (AND HOLY COMMUNION)

A SERVICE OF HYMNS AND READINGS
FOR EASTER SUNDAY EVENING

Easter Day is the festival of all festivals, even more important than
Christmas Day. It is associated with moving from darkness to light, from
death to life, and from hopelessness to hope. Here the truth is revealed that
Christ on the cross has triumphed over death and sins, and that nothing, not
even the tomb, can contain his resurrection power. God has raised him from
the dead. Because the women come to the tomb early and find the body
gone, there is an instinct to begin our celebrations as darkness turns to light:
early in the morning. There is also a long history of baptisms on this day, as
new believers are plunged into the waters, dying to sin, and rising in Christ.
A day to celebrate new life!

AN EASTER EVE SERVICE OF LIGHT AND RENEWAL OF BAPTISMAL PROMISES

The presiding minister may say:
Dear brothers and sisters in Christ,
on this most holy night,
when our Lord Jesus Christ passed from death to life,
the Church invites her children throughout the world
to come together in vigil and prayer.
This is the Passover of the Lord.
We remember his death and resurrection
by hearing his word and celebrating his mysteries,
confident that we shall share in his victory over death
and live with him for ever in God. [12]

When the new fire is kindled:
Eternal God,
Who made this most holy night
to shine with the brightness of your one true light:
set us aflame with the fire of your love,
and bring us to the radiance of your heavenly glory,
through Jesus Christ our Lord. **Amen.** [13]

The Easter candle may be marked
Christ yesterday and today,
the beginning and the end,
Alpha and Omega,
all time belongs to him,
and all ages;
to him be glory and power
through every age and for ever. **Amen.**

The presiding minister lights the Easter Candle, saying:
May the light of Christ, rising in glory,
banish all darkness from our hearts and minds.
The Easter Candle is carried among the congregation and raised at
three points, with the words:
The light of Christ
Thanks be to God.

THE EXSULTET

Sing, choirs of heaven! Let saints and angels sing!
Around God's throne exult in harmony!
Now Jesus Christ is risen from the grave!
Salute your King in glorious symphony!

Sing, choirs of earth! Behold, your light has come!
The glory of the Lord shines radiantly!
Lift up your hearts, for Christ has conquered death!
The night is past, the day of life is here!

Sing, Church of God! Exult with joy outpoured!
The gospel trumpets tell of victory won!
Your Saviour lives, he's with you evermore!
Let all God's people sound the long Amen! [14]

INTRODUCTION

The minister continues

The Lord be with you
and also with you.
Lift up your hearts.
We lift them to the Lord.
Let us give thanks to the Lord our God.
It is right to give our thanks and praise.

It is right and good that with hearts and minds and voices
we should praise you, Father almighty, the unseen God,
through your only Son, Jesus Christ our Lord,
who has saved us by his death,
paid the price of Adam's sin,
and reconciled us once again to you.
Glory to you for ever.

For this is the Passover feast,
when Christ, the true Lamb of God, is slain
whose blood consecrates the homes of all the faithful.
Glory to you for ever.

This is the night when you first saved our ancestors,
freeing Israel from her slavery
and leading her safely through the sea.
Glory to you for ever.

This is the night when Jesus Christ vanquished hell,
broke the chains of death
and rose triumphant from the grave.
Glory to you for ever.

This is the night when all who believe in him are freed from sin,
restored to grace and holiness,
and share the victory of Christ.
Glory to you for ever.

This is the night that gave us back what we had lost;
beyond our deepest dreams
You even made our sin a happy fault.
Glory to you for ever.

Most blessed of all nights!
Evil and hatred are put to flight and sin is washed away,
lost innocence regained, and mourning turned to joy.
Glory to you for ever.

Night truly blessed, when hatred is cast out,
Peace and justice find a home, and heaven is joined to earth and all
creation reconciled to you.
Glory to you for ever.

Therefore, heavenly Father, in this our Easter joy
accept our sacrifice of praise, your Church's solemn offering.
Grant that this Easter candle may make our darkness light.

For Christ the morning star has risen in glory;
Christ is risen from the dead and his flame of love still burns within us!
Christ sheds his peaceful light on all the world!
Christ lives and reigns for ever and ever!
Amen. [15]

AN EASTER EVE SERVICE OF LIGHT AND RENEWAL OF BAPTISMAL PROMISES

THE VIGIL

A hymn may be sung during which lights are taken from the Easter candle to illuminate the Bible from which the vigil readings will be read. The list of Vigil Readings may be found on p.40 of the Book of Common Prayer 2004.

THE EASTER ACCLAMATION

Christ is risen!
The Lord is risen indeed. Alleluia!

GLORIA IN EXCELSIS

Or another Easter song, when the candles of all those present are lit.

THE RENEWAL OF BAPTISMAL VOWS

As we celebrate again the death and resurrection of our Lord Jesus Christ we remember that through these saving acts we have died and been buried with him in baptism, so that we might rise with him to a new life within the family of his Church.
We now meet to renew the promises made at our baptism, to affirm our allegiance to Christ and our rejection of all that is evil.

Do you renew and affirm the promises made at your baptism?
I do.

Do you reject the devil and all proud rebellion against God?
I reject them.
Do you renounce the deceit and corruption of evil?
I renounce them.
Do you repent of the sins that separate us from God and neighbour?
I repent of them.

Do you turn to Christ as Saviour?
I turn to Christ.
Do you submit to Christ as Lord?

I submit to Christ.
Do you come to Christ, the Way, the Truth and the Life?
I come to Christ.

Do you believe and trust in God the Father?
I believe in God, the Father almighty,
creator of heaven and earth.

Do you believe and trust in God the Son?
I believe in Jesus Christ, God's only Son, our Lord
who was conceived by the Holy Spirit,
born of the Virgin Mary,
suffered under Pontius Pilate,
was crucified, died and was buried;
he descended to the dead.
On the third day he rose again;
he ascended into heaven,
he is seated at the right hand of the Father,
and he will come again to judge the living and the dead.

Do you believe and trust in God the Holy Spirit?
I believe in the Holy Spirit,
the holy catholic Church,
the forgiveness of sins,
the resurrection of the body
and the life everlasting. Amen.

The minister continues
Those who are baptized are called to worship and serve God.

Will you continue in the apostles' teaching and fellowship, in the
breaking of bread, and in the prayers?
With the help of God, I will.

Will you persevere in resisting evil, and, whenever you fall into sin,
repent and return to the Lord?
With the help of God, I will.

Will you proclaim by word and example
the good news of God in Christ?
With the help of God, I will.

Will you seek and serve Christ in all people,
Loving your neighbour as yourself?
With the help of God, I will.

Will you acknowledge Christ's authority over human society, by prayer
for the world and its leaders,
by defending the weak, and by seeking peace and justice?
With the help of God, I will.

The minister says
Let us pray:

Almighty God,
you have given us the will to do all these things:
Give us the courage and the strength to achieve them
to the honour and glory of your name,
and the good of your Church and people;
through Jesus Christ our Lord,
who lives and reigns with you and the Holy Spirit,
one God, now and for ever. **Amen.**

May Christ dwell in your hearts through faith,
that you may be rooted and grounded in love
and bring forth the fruit of the Spirit. **Amen.**

AN EASTER MORNING
SUNRISE SERVICE

EASTER
GREETING

The Easter greeting may be said several times, and the congregation may be invited to say the Easter greeting to one another.

Christ is risen!
The Lord is risen indeed. Alleluia!

INTRODUCTION

We meet together to welcome the dawn on this Easter morning. This past night is the night when Jesus overcame death, and on this morning, in the clear light of dawn, we see the reality and power of the resurrection. Christ is the light of the world. Because he lives, those who are in him will live eternally.

READING
MATTHEW 28: 1-7A

SONGS OF
EASTER PRAISE

READING
MARK 16: 1-7

EASTER MORNING
PRAYERS

Different people may be designated to lead the prayers, inviting the power of the risen Christ into every area of life. Or those gathered may be invited to break into small groups and pray silently or aloud; or the congregation may be invited to think of one or two areas they would wish to pray for, and to name them aloud.

The following may be used after each section of the prayers:

Risen Christ,
make your presence known.

THE LORD'S
PRAYER

At the end of the prayers, the leader says:

Trusting in the power of the living Christ,
and seeking God's will on earth,
we pray in the power of the Spirit:
Our Father in heaven.... or **Our Father, who art in heaven**

AN EASTER MORNING SUNRISE SERVICE

READING LUKE 24: 1-9

AN EASTER WORD OR TESTIMONY

A Word of proclamation of the resurrection, or a word of testimony to the power of the resurrection in someone's life.

ACCLAMATION

Here are words you may trust.
Remember Jesus Christ, risen from the dead:
he is our salvation, our eternal glory.
If we die with him, we shall live with him:
if we endure, we shall reign with him.
If we deny him, he will deny us:
if we are faithless, he keeps faith.
For he has broken the power of death
and brought life and immortality to light through the gospel. [16]

cf 2 Timothy 2: 11-13

SONGS OF EASTER PRAISE

The people present accompany the first three responses with a sweep of the arm towards a cross, or behind them, as if throwing the objects of prayer; the final response is a sweep of the arm towards the light or towards heaven. The responses are declared firmly.

DISMISSAL

All our problems
we send to the cross of Christ.
All our difficulties
we send to the cross of Christ.
All the devil's works
we send to the cross of Christ.
All our hopes
we set on the risen Christ.
And the blessing of God almighty,
the Father, the Son and the Holy Spirit,
be with you and remain with you,
this Easter Day and always. **Amen.** [17]

Go in the peace of the risen Christ. Alleluia! Alleluia!
Thanks be to God. Alleluia! Alleluia! [18]

A SERVICE OF THE WORD
(AND HOLY COMMUNION)
FOR EASTER DAY

Christ is risen!
The Lord is risen indeed. Alleluia!

This greeting is acclaimed rather than just spoken and may be repeated at appropriate points throughout the service.

The minister continues:
Praise be to the God and Father of our Lord Jesus Christ.
In his great mercy we have been born again into a living hope through the resurrection of Jesus Christ from the dead.
Praise be to the God and Father of our Lord Jesus Christ.
He has blessed us with every spiritual blessing in the heavenly places.
Christ is risen!
He is risen indeed. Alleluia!

This is the day when our Lord Jesus Christ was raised gloriously from the dead, crushing the power of sin and destroying the sting of death. Throughout the world, Christians celebrate the mighty power of God, as Christ calls us out of darkness to share in his marvellous light. May we, and all Christ's people, shine as lights in the world, to the glory of God the Father.

The minister may light the Easter candle, saying:
May the light of Christ, rising in glory
banish all darkness from our hearts and minds.
The light of Christ
Thanks be to God. [19]

**THE COLLECT
OF THE DAY**

Almighty God,
through your only-begotten Son Jesus Christ
you have overcome death
and opened to us the gate of everlasting life:
Grant that, as by your grace going before us,
you put into our minds good desires,
so by your continual help we may bring them to good effect;
through Jesus Christ our risen Lord
who is alive and reigns with you and the Holy Spirit,
one God, now and for ever. **Amen.**

PROCLAIMING AND RECEIVING THE WORD

READINGS

Either one or two readings from scripture precede the Gospel reading.

EASTER ANTHEMS

**Christ our Passover has been sacrificed for us:
therefore let us celebrate the feast,
not with the old leaven of corruption and wickedness:
but with the unleavened bread of sincerity and truth.
Christ, once raised from the dead, dies no more;
death has no more dominion over him.
In dying, he died to sin once and for all;
in living, he lives to God.
See yourselves, therefore, as dead to sin:
and alive to God in Jesus Christ our Lord.
Christ has been raised from the dead:
the firstfruits of those who sleep.
For as by man came death:
by man has come also the resurrection of the dead.
for as in Adam all die, even so in Christ shall all be made alive.
Glory to the Father, and to the Son, and to the Holy Spirit:
as it was in the beginning, is now, and shall be for ever. Amen.**

**THE EASTER
GOSPEL**

may be introduced by the following acclamation:
Jesus Christ is risen from the dead:
Alleluia!
He has defeated the powers of death:

Alleluia!
Jesus turns our sorrow into dancing:
Alleluia!
He has the words of eternal life:
Alleluia! [20]

Hear the gospel of our Saviour Christ according to....
Glory to you, Lord Jesus Christ.
At the end:
This is the Gospel of the risen Lord:
Praise to you, Lord Jesus Christ.

SERMON

AFFIRMATION
OF FAITH

Let us declare our faith in the resurrection of Jesus Christ:
Christ died for our sins
in accordance with the Scriptures;
he was buried;
he was raised to life on the third day
in accordance with the Scriptures;
afterwards he appeared to his followers,
and to all the apostles:
this we have received,
and this we believe. Amen [21]
cf 1 Corinthians 15: 3-7

THE PRAYERS OF THE PEOPLE

We pray to Jesus who is present with us to eternity.

Jesus, light of the world,
bring the light and peace of your gospel to the nations.....
Jesus, Lord of life,
in your mercy, hear us.

Jesus, bread of life,
give food to the hungry...

and nourish us all with your word.
Jesus, Lord of life
in your mercy, hear us.

Jesus, our way, our truth, our life,
be with us and all who follow you in the way.....
Deepen our appreciation of your truth
and fill us with your life.
Jesus, Lord of life,
in your mercy, hear us.

Jesus, Good Shepherd who gave your life for the sheep,
recover the straggler,
bind up the injured,
strengthen the sick
and lead the healthy and strong to new pastures.
Jesus, Lord of life,
in your mercy hear us.

Jesus, the resurrection and the life,
we give you thanks for all who have lived and believed in you....
Raise us with them to eternal life.
Jesus, Lord of life,
in your mercy, hear us,
accept our prayers, and be with us always. Amen. [22]

THE PEACE

The risen Christ came and stood among his disciples and said,
Peace be with you.
Then they were glad when they saw the Lord.
The peace of the risen Lord be always with you:
and also with you.

CELEBRATING AT THE LORD'S TABLE

Be present, be present,
Lord Jesus Christ our risen high priest;
make yourself known in the breaking of bread. **Amen.**

Stand
The bishop or priest who presides takes the bread and wine and may say
Christ our passover has been sacrificed for us
therefore let us celebrate the feast.

The Eucharistic Prayer is said by the presiding minister:
The Lord is here.
His Spirit is with us.

Lift up your hearts.
We lift them to the Lord.
Let us give thanks to the Lord our God.
It is right to give our thanks and praise.
Father, almighty and everliving God,
at all times and in all places
it is right to give you thanks and praise:

Above all we praise you
for the glorious resurrection of your Son
Jesus Christ our Lord,
the true paschal lamb who was sacrificed for us;
by dying he destroyed our death;
by rising he restored our life:

And so with all your people,
with angels and archangels,
and with all the company of heaven,
we proclaim your great and glorious name,
for ever praising you and saying:
Holy, holy, holy Lord,
God of power and might,
heaven and earth are full of your glory.
Hosanna in the highest!

Blessed is he who comes in the name of the Lord.
Hosanna in the highest!

Blessed are you, Father,
the creator and sustainer of all things;
you made us in your own image,

male and female you created us;
even when we turned away from you,
you never ceased to care for us,
but in your love and mercy you freed us from the slavery of sin,
giving your only begotten Son to become man
and suffer death on the cross to redeem us:
he made there the one complete and all-sufficient sacrifice
for the sins of the whole world:
he instituted,
and in his holy Gospel commanded us to continue,
a perpetual memory of his precious death
until he comes again.

On the night that he was betrayed he took bread;
and when he had given thanks to you, he broke it,
and gave it to his disciples, saying, Take, eat,
this is my body which is given for you.
Do this in remembrance of me.

In the same way, after supper he took the cup;
and when he had given thanks to you,
he gave it to them, saying, Drink this, all of you,
for this is my blood of the new covenant
which is shed for you and for many
for the forgiveness of sins.
Do this, as often as you drink it,
in remembrance of me.

Therefore, Father, with this bread and this cup
we do as Christ your Son commanded:
we remember his passion and death,
we celebrate his resurrection and ascension,
and we look for the coming of his kingdom.

Accept through him, our great high priest,
this our sacrifice of praise and thanksgiving;
and as we eat and drink these holy gifts,
grant by the power of the life-giving Spirit
that we may be made one in your holy Church
and partakers of the body and blood of your Son,
that he may dwell in us and we in him:

Through the same Jesus Christ our Lord,
by whom, and with whom, and in whom,
in the unity of the Holy Spirit,
all honour and glory are yours, Almighty Father,
for ever and ever. Amen.

The presiding minister says
As our Saviour Christ has taught us, so we pray:
Our Father in heaven...
or
As our Saviour Christ has taught us, we are bold to say:
Our Father, who art in heaven....

THE LORD'S
PRAYER

The presiding minister (who may be assisted by the deacon) breaks the
consecrated bread in preparation for the Communion.
Jesus says, I am the bread of life,
whoever eats this bread will live for ever:
Lord, our hearts hunger for you;
give us this bread always. [23]

THE BREAKING
OF THE BREAD

The presiding minister says
Draw near with faith.
Receive the body of our Lord Jesus Christ which he gave for you,
and his blood which he shed for you.
Remember that he died for you, and lives for you
and feed on him in your hearts by faith with thanksgiving.
The presiding minister and people receive communion.

THE COMMUNION

THE GREAT
SILENCE

GOING OUT AS GOD'S PEOPLE

PRAYER AFTER COMMUNION

Living God,
For our redemption you gave your only begotten Son
To the death of the cross,
And by his glorious resurrection
You have delivered us from the power of our enemy.
Grant us so to die daily unto sin,
That we may evermore live with him in the joy of his risen life;
Through Jesus Christ our Lord.

All say
**Almighty God,
we thank you for feeding us
with the spiritual food
of the body and blood of your Son Jesus Christ.
Through him we offer you our souls and bodies
to be a living sacrifice.
Send us out in the power of your Spirit
to live and work to your praise and glory. Amen.**

DISMISSAL

God the Father,
by whose love Christ was raised from the dead,
open to you who believe the gates of everlasting life.
Amen.

God the Son,
who in bursting from the grave has won a glorious victory,
give you joy as you share the Easter faith.
Amen.

God the Holy Spirit,
who filled the disciples with the life of the risen Christ,
empower you and fill you with Christ's peace.
Amen.

And the blessing of God almighty....

Go in the peace of the risen Christ. Alleluia! Alleluia!
Thanks be to God. Alleluia! Alleluia!

A SERVICE OF HYMNS AND READINGS

FOR EASTER SUNDAY EVENING

Meetings with the Risen Christ

Christ is risen
The Lord is risen indeed. Alleluia!

The Easter Greeting may be repeated at the beginning of each section.

EASTER GREETING

OPENING HYMN

Living God,
for our redemption you gave your only-begotten Son
to the death of the cross,
and by his glorious resurrection
you have delivered us from the power of our enemy.
Grant us so to die daily to sin,
that we may evermore live with him
in the joy of his risen life,
through Jesus Christ our Lord. **Amen.**

COLLECT OF
EASTER DAY

Christ our Passover has been sacrificed for us:
Therefore let us celebrate the feast,
not with the old leaven of corruption and wickedness,
but with the unleavened bread of sincerity and truth.
Christ, once raised from the dead, dies no more;
death has no more dominion over him.
In dying, he died to sin once for all,
in living, he lives to God.
See yourselves, therefore, as dead to sin;
and alive to God in Jesus Christ our Lord.
Christ has been raised from the dead,
The first-fruits of those who sleep.
For as by man came death,
by man has come also the resurrection of the dead.
For as in Adam all die,
even so in Christ shall all be made alive.
Glory to the Father and to the Son, and to the Holy Spirit:
as it was in the beginning, is now and shall be for ever. Amen.

THE EASTER
ANTHEMS

A SERVICE OF HYMNS AND READINGS FOR EASTER SUNDAY EVENING

THE READINGS AND HYMNS

MATTHEW 28: 1-10	1. The meeting with the women at the tomb
HYMN	
LUKE 24: 13-27	2. The meeting on the Emmaus Road
HYMN	
LUKE 24: 33-49	3. The meeting with the other disciples
HYMN	
JOHN 20: 19-23	4. The commissioning of the disciples
HYMN	
JOHN 20: 24-29	5. The meeting with Thomas
HYMN	
JOHN 21: 9-14	6. The meeting at the Lakeside
HYMN	

7. The confrontation of Peter

JOHN 21: 15-19

HYMN

8. Jesus and the beloved disciple

JOHN 21: 20-25

HYMN

THE LORD'S
PRAYER

THE EASTER
BLESSING

God the Father,
by whose love Christ was raised from the dead,
open to you who believe the gates of everlasting life.
Amen.

God the Son,
who in bursting from the grave has won a glorious victory,
give you joy as you share the Easter faith.
Amen.

God the Holy Spirit,
Who filled the disciples with the life of the risen Lord,
Empower you and fill you with Christ's peace.
Amen.

And the blessing of God almighty,
the Father, the Son and the Holy Spirit,
be with you this Easter day and for evermore. **Amen.**

Go in the peace of the risen Christ. Alleluia! Alleluia!
Thanks be to God. Alleluia! Alleluia!

DISMISSAL

HOLY WEEK RESOURCES

1. DRAMATIZED READINGS OF THE PASSION

The Gospel is introduced with the words:
The Passion of our Lord Jesus Christ, according to *N*

When the reading comes to the place where the crowd shouts for the crucifixion of Jesus, the whole congregation is asked to stand, if not already standing, and join in the parts in bold.

Matthew 27: 17ff NRSV
...So after they had gathered, Pilate said to them, 'Who do you want me to release for you? Jesus Barabbas or Jesus who is called the Messiah?' For he realized that it was out of jealousy that they had handed him over. While he was sitting on the judgement seat his wife sent word to him, 'Have nothing to do with that innocent man, for today I have suffered a great deal because of a dream about him.' Now the chief priests and the elders persuaded the crowds to ask for Barabbas and to have Jesus killed. The governor again said to them, 'Which of the two do you want me to release for you?'

And they said,
(Loudly)
'Barabbas.'
Then what should I do with Jesus who is called the Messiah?' All of them said,
(Loudly)
'Let him be crucified!'
Then he asked 'Why, what evil has he done?'
But they shouted all the more,
(Even more loudly)
'LET HIM BE CRUCIFIED!'...
or Mark 15: 6ff NRSV

...Now at the festival he used to release a prisoner for them, anyone for whom they asked. Now a man called Barabbas was in prison with the rebels who had committed murder during the insurrection. So the crowd came and began to ask Pilate to do for them according to his custom. Then he answered them, 'Do you want me to release for you the King of the Jews?' For he realized that it was out of jealousy that the chief priests had handed him over. But the chief priests stirred up the crowd to have him release Barabbas for them instead. Pilate spoke to them again 'Then what do you wish me to do with the man you call the King of the Jews?' They shouted back,

(Loudly)
'Crucify him!'.
Pilate asked them, 'Why, what evil has he done? But they shouted all the more
(Even more loudly)
'CRUCIFY HIM!'
So Pilate, wishing to satisfy the crowd, released Barabbas for them; and after flogging
Jesus, he handed him over to be crucified.
or **Luke 23: 13ff NRSV**

...Pilate then called together the chief priests, the leaders and the people, and said to
them, 'You brought me this man as the one who was perverting the people; and here I
have examined him in your presence and have not found this man guilty of any of your
charges against him. Neither has Herod, for he sent him back to us. Indeed, he has done
nothing to deserve death. I will therefore have him flogged and release him.'

Then they shouted out together,
(Loudly)
'Away with this fellow! Release Barabbas for us!'
(This was a man who had been put in prison for an insurrection that had taken place in
the city and for murder). Pilate, wanting to release Jesus, addressed them again, but they
kept shouting,
(Even more loudly)
'CRUCIFY HIM!'
A third time he said to them, 'Why, what evil has he done? I have found in him no ground
for the sentence of death; I will therefore have him flogged and then release him.' But
they kept urgently demanding with loud shouts that he should be crucified.....

At the end, the reader says
This is the Passion of the Lord.

A period of silence is kept for reflection

2. INTERCESSIONS

Lord Jesus, on this day you entered into Jerusalem to fulfil your Father's will:
give us grace to enter into your will and purpose for our lives.
Lord, hear us
Lord, graciously hear us.

Lord Jesus, on this day you began a journey which would lead to pain and suffering:
give grace to those who are on difficult journeys in their own lives.
Lord, hear us
Lord, graciously hear us.

Lord Jesus, on this day you received the welcome and acclamation of the crowds:
keep us pure in heart when we receive praise and encouragement.
Lord, hear us
Lord, graciously hear us.

Lord Jesus, on this day you rode in humility on a donkey:
keep us from exalting ourselves, and make us humble in everything we do.
Lord, hear us
Lord, graciously hear us.

Lord Jesus, on this day, the people sang praise with all their strength:
make our praises joyful, but always from the depth of our hearts.
Lord, hear us
Lord, graciously hear us.

Lord Jesus, on this day, the cold jealousy of the Pharisees is exposed, as they want the people to stop:
forgive us when the praise of others shows up our coldness of heart.
Lord, hear us
Lord, graciously hear us.

Lord Jesus, on this day, you said the very stones might sing your praise:
give us such a reverence for your creation that we may sing our praises in harmony with all you have made.
Lord, hear us
Lord, graciously hear us.

Lord Jesus, on this day you wept for the peace of Jerusalem, your beloved city.
We pray for the peace of that holy place, and for peace in our own towns and cities.
Lord, hear us
Lord, graciously hear us.

Lord Jesus, on this day many did not recognize that they were being visited by the Son of God:
open our hearts and minds that we may recognize you in all your words, works and ways.
Lord, hear us
Lord, graciously hear us.

In offering our prayers this Palm Sunday, we commit ourselves to follow you on the way to
the cross, in the knowledge that this way is none other than the way of life and peace.
Lord Jesus, be our Way
Lord Jesus, be our Truth,
Lord Jesus, be our Life,
this Holy Week and for ever. Amen

B. HOLY WEEK INTERCESSION 1 [24]

Let us bring to our Father our prayers of intercession through Christ who gave himself for
the life of the world.

For forgiveness for the many times we have denied Jesus,
let us pray to the Lord.
Lord, have mercy

For grace to seek out those habits of sin which mean spiritual death and by prayer and
self-discipline to overcome them,
let us pray to the Lord.
Lord, have mercy.

For Christian people, that through the suffering of disunity there may grow a rich union in
Christ,
let us pray to the Lord.
Lord, have mercy.

For those who make laws, interpret them and administer them,
that our common life may be ordered in justice and mercy,

let us pray to the Lord.
Lord, have mercy.

For those who still make Jerusalem a battleground,
let us pray to the Lord.
Lord, have mercy.

For those who have the courage and honesty to work openly for justice and peace,
let us pray to the Lord.
Lord, have mercy.

For those in the darkness and agony of isolation, that they may find support and
encouragement,
let us pray to the Lord.
Lord, have mercy.

For those who, weighed down with hardship, failure or sorrow, feel that God is far from them,
let us pray to the Lord.
Lord, have mercy.

For those who are tempted to give up the way of the cross,
let us pray to the Lord.
Lord, have mercy.

That we, with those who have died in faith, may find mercy in the day of Christ,
let us pray to the Lord.
Lord, have mercy.

Holy God,
holy and strong,
holy and immortal,
have mercy on us.

C. HOLY WEEK INTERCESSION 2 [25]

Let us pray to the Father through his Son
who suffered on the cross for the world's redemption.

Fill with your Spirit Christ's broken body, the Church...

Give to Christian people everywhere a deep longing
to take up the cross and to understand its mysterious glory.
By the Saviour's cross and passion,
Lord, save us and help us.

Bless those who lead the Church's worship at this solemn time...
In the preaching of the word and the celebration of the sacraments draw your people
close to you.
By the Saviour's cross and passion,
Lord, save us and help us.

Strengthen those who are preparing for baptism,
together with their teachers, sponsors and families...
Teach them what it means to die and rise with Christ
and prepare them to receive the breath of his Spirit.
By the Saviour's cross and passion,
Lord, save us and help us.

Look in your mercy on the world you loved so much
that you sent your Son to suffer and to die....
Strengthen those who work to share
the reconciliation won at such cost upon the cross.
By the Saviour's cross and passion,
Lord, save us and help us.

Bring healing by the wounds of Christ
To all who are weighed down by pain and injustice....
Help the lonely and the betrayed, the suffering and the dying, to find strength in the
companionship of Jesus,
and in his passion to know their salvation.
By the Saviour's cross and passion,
Lord, save us and help us.

Welcome us into paradise when we leave this world in your friendship.
According to your promises bring us with all your saints
to share in all the benefits of Christ's death and resurrection.
By the Saviour's cross and passion,
Lord, save us and help us.

Holy God,
holy and strong,

holy and immortal,
have mercy on us.

D. HOLY WEEK INTERCESSION 3 [26]

Let us pray to the Father, who loved the world so much that he sent his only Son to give us life.

Simon from Cyrene was forced to carry the cross for your Son.
Give us grace to lift heavy loads from those we meet
and to stand with those condemned to die.
Lord, hear us.
Lord, graciously hear us.

Your Son watched the soldiers gamble to share his clothes.
Transform the hearts of those who make a profit from their victims, and those whose
hearts are hardened by their work.
Lord, hear us.
Lord, graciously hear us.

The thief, who was crucified by Jesus,
was promised a place in your kingdom.
Give pardon and hope, healing and peace
to all who look death in the face.
Lord, hear us.
Lord, graciously hear us.

From the cross Jesus entrusted Mary his mother
and John his disciple to each other's care.
Help us also to care for one another
and fill our homes with the spirit of your love.
Lord, hear us.
Lord, graciously hear us.

In Mary and John your Son created a new family at the cross.
Fill our relationships and those of new families today,
with mutual care and responsibility, and give us a secure hope for the future.
Lord, hear us.
Lord, graciously hear us.

The centurion was astonished to see your glory in the crucified Messiah.

Open the eyes of those who do not know you
to see your Son in the meaning of life and death.
Lord, hear us.
Lord, graciously hear us.

Joseph of Arimathea came to take your Son's body away.
Give hope and faith to the dying and bereaved,
and gentleness to those who minister to them.
Lord, hear us.
Lord, graciously hear us.

Simon and Joseph, Mary and John
became part of your Church in Jerusalem.
Bring into your Church today a varied company of people,
to walk with Christ in the way of his passion
and to find salvation in the victory of his cross.
Lord of the Church,
hear our prayers,
and make us one in heart and mind
to serve you in Christ our Lord. Amen

E. HOLY WEEK INTERCESSION 4 - AN INTERCESSION ON MINISTRY FOR MAUNDY THURSDAY

God the Father
have mercy on us
God the Son
have mercy on us
God the Holy Spirit
have mercy on us

We humbly pray that you will hear us, good Lord.
Grant to your people the forgiveness of sins,
growth in grace and the fruit of the Spirit.
Lord, hear our prayer

Send your peace to the world
which you have reconciled to yourself

by the ministry of your Son Jesus Christ.
Lord, hear our prayer

Heal the divisions of your Church,
that all may be one
so that the world may believe.
Lord, hear our prayer

Lead the members of your Church
in their vocation and ministry,
that they may serve you in true and godly living.
Lord, hear our prayer

Raise up faithful and able ministers for your Church,
that the Gospel may be known to all people.
Lord, hear our prayer

Fill them with compassion,
clothe them with humility,
and move them to care for all your people.
Lord, hear our prayer

Inspire all bishops, priests and deacons with your love,
that with all your people they may hunger for truth.
Lord, hear our prayer

Sustain by the indwelling of your Holy Spirit
all who are called to the ordained ministries of your Church
and encourage them to persevere to the end.
Lord, hear our prayer

Gather us with all your saints into your eternal kingdom.
Lord, hear our prayer

Eternal God and Father,
you have promised to hear those who pray
in the name of your Son:
Grant that what we have asked in faith
we may obtain according to your will;
through Jesus Christ our Lord. Amen

3. READINGS APPROPRIATE TO THE WATCH

Which may be read as silent personal devotion
or, gently but publicly, at intervals during the time.

John 13: 16-30
Psalm 113

John 13: 31-end
Psalm 114

John 14: 1-14
Psalm 115

John 14: 15-end
Psalm 116: 1-9

John 15: 1-17
Psalm 116: 10-end

John 15: 18-16: 4a
Psalm 117

John 16: 4b-15
Psalm 118: 1-9

John 16: 16-end
Psalm 118: 10-18

John 17: 1-19
Psalm 118: 19-end

John 17: 20-end

REFERENCES

[1] From *Common Worship: Times and Seasons* (2006), p.277. © The Archbishops' Council 2006

[2] From *Believing We Pray: Daily Prayer for Lent and Easter Year B*, p.42. © Brian Mayne, reproduced here by permission of The Columba Press

[3] From *Common Worship: Times and Seasons* (2006) op. cit., p.272

[4] From *Handbook of the Christian Year* (1986), p.161. © Abingdon Press

[5] From *Common Worship: Times and Seasons* (2006) op. cit., p.297

[6] ibid., p.298

[7] ibid., p.299

[8] ibid., p.300

[9] ibid., p.304

[10] Based on an idea by Martin Payne on the Bible reading Fellowship website (*www.brf.org.uk*)

[11] From *New Handbook of the Christian Year* (1992). © Abingdon Press 1992, appearing in *Common Worship: Times and Seasons* (2006) op. cit., p.310

[12] From *Common Worship: Times and Seasons* (2006) op. cit., p.334

[13] ibid.,

[14] ibid., p.336

[15] ibid., p.337

[16] Ibid., p.441

[17] © Modern Services, Uzima Press (1991), appearing in Common Worship: Times and Seasons (2006) op. cit., p.407

[18] From *Common Worship: Times and Seasons* (2006) op. cit., p.407

[19] ibid., p.402

[20] ibid., p.431

[21] From New Patterns for Worship (2008), p.165. © The Archbishops' Council 2008

[22] From *Common Worship: Times and Seasons* (2006) op. cit., p.433

[23] ibid., p.369

[24] ibid., p.261

[25] © Michael Perham, appearing in *Common Worship: Times and Seasons* (2006) op. cit., p.263

[26] © Trevor Lloyd, appearing in *Common Worship: Times and Seasons* (2006) op. cit., p.264